gratitude

VIRTUES OF MY HEART

Written and Illustrated by Melissa López Charepoo

Text and Illustrations
©2023 Melissa López Charepoo

First published 2023. Reprint 2026.

ISBN 978-1-971750-29-3 (paperback)

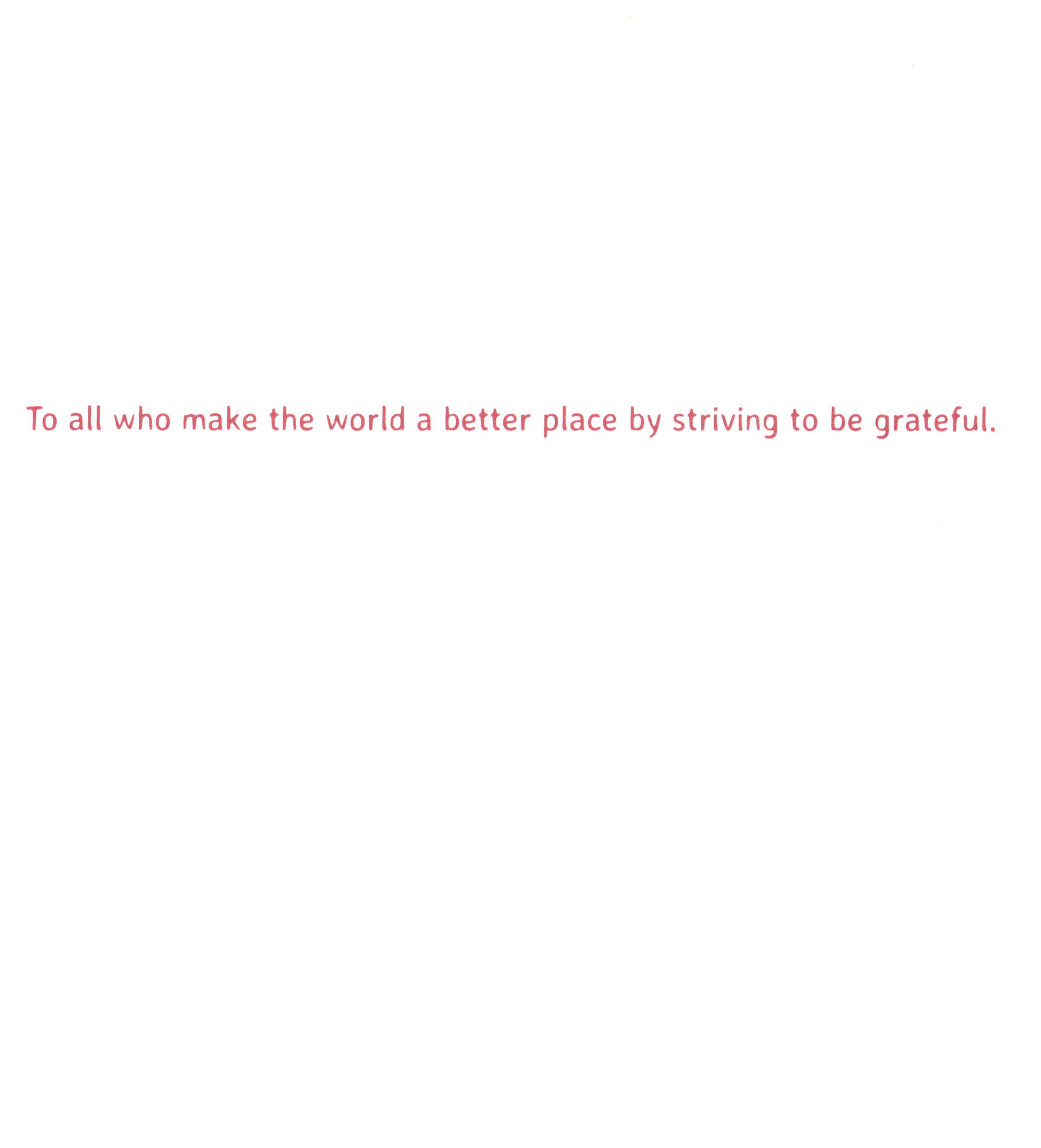
To all who make the world a better place by striving to be grateful.

Have you ever wondered what it means to have **gratitude**?

Gratitude is the act of being thankful and being able to appreciate everything in life. It's a virtue, or a good quality of our hearts. Being grateful makes our hearts joyful and helps us develop many other virtues as well. We should be grateful to our Creator, our parents, and anyone who serves our community. We can also be grateful for our toys and the fun things we get to do. We are truly happy when we are grateful.

We can strive to be grateful for everything in life!

My heart is full of gratitude for our Creator. I'm thankful for everything He has given me. I trust, have **faith**, and believe that He guides my steps every single day. To strive for gratitude towards our Creator, I pray every day and meditate on His Word.

How do you show gratitude towards our Creator?

My heart is full of gratitude for my family, especially my parents. I am grateful for everything they do and everything they have taught me. I show my gratitude to them by being **obedient**. I strive to complete my chores every day. I always follow their guidance, as I know they want the best for me.

How do you strive for gratitude by being **obedient** to your parents or grownups in your life?

My heart is full of gratitude for spiritual gifts, like the kindness shown to me by others, and material gifts, such as my soccer ball and my special journal. I'm grateful I get to enjoy those things in life, but I'm also **detached** from them. That means I don't allow the need to have those things control me. Sometimes we come across kind people, and sometimes we don't. The same goes for material things. Sometimes we have them, and sometimes we don't. By being **detached**, I feel grateful either way.

How do you strive to be grateful while also being **detached**?

My heart is full of gratitude for the things I can learn. At school, I strive to pay attention and finish all my work. At home I strive for gratitude by **sacrificing** my time of watching my favorite show to make sure I complete all my homework.

What are some things you are grateful for? What do you need to **sacrifice** to achieve them?

My heart is full of gratitude for my friends. I show them how grateful I am to have them in my life by always **respecting** them, even though we may have differences in our opinions. I make sure that I listen carefully to what they have to say.

What are some of the things you can do to be grateful for your friends by showing them **respect**?

My heart is full of gratitude for test and difficulties. It could be hard to be grateful for difficult things in life. However, when things in life get difficult, it helps us develop virtues and become stronger and better people. Life will always have its ups and downs. But having a grateful heart makes us **resilient**, as it gives us the capacity to quickly recover from difficult times. Having a grateful heart also gives us **optimism** as we look forward to better times. The other day my team lost a soccer match, but we are **resilient**, and we are **optimistic** that we will win again with effort and practice.

How do you show gratitude by striving to be **resilient** and **optimistic** during difficult times?

My heart is full of gratitude for everyone who serves our community. Many good teachers, police officers, firefighters, doctors, and nurses, among many others, serve our community with responsibility and care. I show my **appreciation** for their work by treating them with **kindness** and **respect**, just as I hope they treat me. People who serve others inspire me to do the same, and I hope in the future to choose a profession that will serve my community.

How do you show gratitude by **appreciating** the work of those who serve our community?

My heart is full of gratitude to our Creator for the beautiful world He made for us. I show my gratitude to planet earth by **caring** for it so that everyone can enjoy this beautiful place we all call home.

How do show gratitude toward our Creator by taking **care** of our planet?

As you can see, we can strive to always have our hearts full of **gratitude**. By having **gratitude**, our hearts develop many other virtues, such as faith, love, mindfulness, detachment, sacrifice, respect, resilience, optimism, service, appreciation, and caring.

Our hearts will always be joyful when we strive to show **gratitude** every day of our lives!

Glossary

Appreciation - recognition and enjoyment of the good qualities in someone or something

Caring - showing kindness and concern for others

Detachment - the ability to accept the things we can't control or change

Faith - having deep trust in our Creator

Love - deep affection towards someone

Mindfulness – being aware of our actions, words, and thoughts, and what surround us

Obedience - compliance with an order, request, or law

Optimism - ability to look for the positive in every situation

Resilience - capacity to recover quickly from difficulties

Respect - a deep admiration for someone or something

Sacrifice – ability to give up something important for something more important

Service - the act of helping others without expecting anything in return

References:

The Virtues Project Cards

Oxford English Dictionary

Heartfelt thanks to:

My beloved husband Darioush Charepoo for all his support.

Our dearly loved boys for being the inspiration.

Leanna Guillén Mora for helping with proofreading and editing the book.

www.ingramcontent.com/pod-product-compliance
Lightning Source LLC
Chambersburg PA
CBHW042159030726
47599CB00004B/792